# Bakewell
# - a visitors guide

## by

## JOHN N. MERRILL

**TRAIL CREST PUBLICATIONS Ltd.,**
*- "from footprint to finished book."*

## 1994

Sandia Mountains
New Mexico. USA

# TRAIL CREST
# PUBLICATIONS
## Ltd.,

Milne House,
Speedwell Mill,
Miller's Green,
Wirksworth,
Derbyshire
DE4 4BL

**(0629) 826354**
**(0629) 826354**

Edited, typeset, designed, paged, printed, marketed and distributed by John N. Merrill.

© Text, walks, Maps, sketches
John N. Merrill/Suncrest Ventures Ltd. 1994.

First Published - June 1994

ISBN 1 874754 33 0

*U.S.A.*
*office -*
*P.O. Box 124,*
*Santa Rosa,*
*New Mexico*
*88435*
*U.S.A.*

**Please note** - The maps in this guide are purely illustrative. You are encouraged to use the appropriate 1:25,000 O.S. map.

Meticulous research has been undertaken to ensure that this publication is highly accurate at the time of going to press. The publishers, however, cannot be held responsible for alterations, errors or omissions, but they would welcome notification of such for future editions.

Typeset in - Times - bold, italic and plain 11pt and 18pt.

Printed by - Footprint Press Ltd./John N. Merrill at Milne House, Speedwell Mill, Miller's Green, Wirksworth, Derbyshire. DE4 4BL.
Cover sketch " River Wye Bridge, Bakewell
© Suncrest Ventures Ltd. 1994.

An all British
product.

# CONTENTS

# ABOUT
# JOHN N. MERRILL

Born in the flatlands of Bedfordshire he soon moved to Sheffield and discovered the joy of the countryside in the Peak District, where he lives. A keen walker who travels the world exploring mountains and trails. Over the last twenty years he has walked more than 150,000 miles - including the first walk around the entire coastline of Britain, 7,000 miles - and worn out over seventy pairs of boots. He has written more than 120 walk guides to areas in Britain and abroad, and created numerous challenge walks which have been used to raise more than £500,000 for charity. New Mexico, USA is his second home.

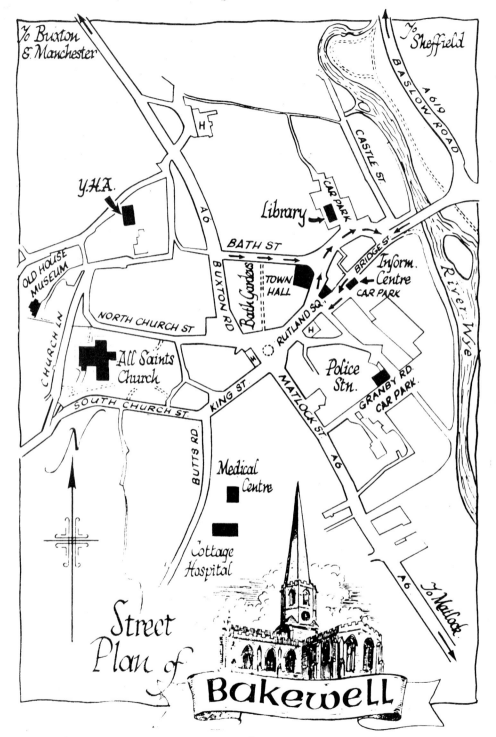

To Buxton & Manchester

To Sheffield

A619 BASLOW ROAD

CASTLE ST

Y.H.A.

Library

CAR PARK

OLD HOUSE MUSEUM

BATH ST

A6

BUXTON RD

Bath Gardens

TOWN HALL

BRIDGE ST

Inform. Centre

CAR PARK

River Wye

CHURCH LN

NORTH CHURCH ST

RUTLAND SQ.

All Saints Church

Police Stn.

GRANBY RD CAR PARK

SOUTH CHURCH ST

KING ST

MATLOCK ST

A6

BUTTS RD

Medical Centre

Cottage Hospital

Street Plan of Bakewell

To Matlock

A6

# INTRODUCTION

Bakewell is the largest and most important town within the boundaries of the Peak District National Park. Although an administrative centre for the National Park, the town has several industries, holds a large agricultural market every week and is immortalised by its famous puddings. The town has numerous historical buildings, customs, traditions and enchanting walks, while the surrounding countryside is extremely rich in interest and very diverse in its make up. To the east lies the gritstone edge country, and at the three other points of the compass are unforgettable limestone dales and villages. All are fascinating, with a long history and where numerous customs are still practised today. Within three miles of the town are two of England's finest buildings - Chatsworth House and Haddon Hall.

All this means that Bakewell is the premier base for exploring - either on foot or by car - one of England's finest pieces of countryside. To help you in this the town has ample facilities for the visitor - several hotels, guest houses, a Youth Hostel, camp and caravan sites close by, an Information Centre, a regular bus service to the outlying villages and a comprehensive shopping area. All in all a better base for getting to know the area would be hard to find.

*Happy exploring and walking!*
*John N. Merrill*

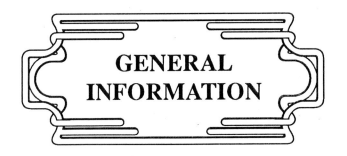

# GENERAL INFORMATION

**BAKEWELL** is in the county of Derbyshire and lies centrally within the Peak District National Park. It is 152 miles from London, 33 miles from Manchester, 25 miles from Derby, 12 miles from Buxton and Chesterfield, and 10 miles from Matlock. Being situated on the A6 trunk road access to the town is straightforward. From the south via Derby and from the north via Buxton, the A6 brings you to the centre of the town. From the east, from Sheffield the A621 brings you to Baslow where the A619 leads to Bakewell. From Chesterfield and the Ml, the A619 takes you via Baslow to Bakewell. Monday is market day and the town becomes very congested.

**Population:** approx. 5,000

**Area of Parish District:** 3,061 acres. Part of the Derbyshire Dales District Council.

**Early Closing day:** Thursday.

**Ordnance Survey Map** showing Bakewell and its surrounding area:
- 1:50,000 series Sheet No. 119 — "Buxton, Matlock and Dovedale".
- 1:25,000 Outdoor Leisure Series - The White Peak - East sheet.

Rainfall: Yearly average 40 inches.

New Street; off Coombs Road; behind Old Market Hall; Granby Road.

Market Place; Rutland Recreation Ground.

Old Market Hall, Bridge Street. Tel. 0629 - 813227. Local Bed Booking Service.

**Police Station:** Granby Road, Tel. Bakewell 812504.

**Public Library:** New Street, Tel. Bakewell 812267.

**Post Office:** Tel. Bakewell 812978.

**Banks:** TSB, Midland, National Westminster, Royal Bank of Scotland. All in or adjacent to The Square.

**Churches:** Church of England: All Saints, South Church Street. Holy Communion 8 a.m., Matins 11 a.m., Evensong 6-30 p.m. Church of the English Martyrs, Buxton Road. Morning Mass 9 a.m. Friends' Meeting House, Dagnall Terrace, Matlock Street. Methodist Church, Matlock Street, 10-45 a.m. and 6-30 p.m. Plymouth Brethren's Meeting Room, Oddfellows' Hall, 11 a.m. and 6-30 p.m. Wesleyan Reform Church, Bagshawe Hill, Buxton Road, 2-30 p.m.

**Caravan Sites:** Newhaven Caravan and Camping Park, Newhaven. Tel. Hartington 300.
Greenhills Caravan Park, Crow Hill Lane, Bakewell. Tel 0629 - 81346
Harthill Hall Caravan Site, Harthill. Tel 0629 - 86203

**Camping Sites:** Haddon Grove Camping Site, Over Haddon, Tel. Bakewell 812343;
Mill Farm—Miss A. Marsden, Haddon Grove, Over Haddon.
Mrs. J. W. Bailey, Dudwood House, Winster;

**Youth Hostel:** Bakewell—Fly Hill, Tel. Bakewell 812313.

**Bed and Breakfast:**
Everton, Haddon Road, Bakewell. Tel 0629 - 813725
Avenue House, Haddon Road, Bakewell. Tel. 0629 - 812467.
Bubnell Cliff Farm, Wheatlands Lane, Baslow. Tel. 0246 - 582454
Castle Farm, Middleton by Youlgreave. Tel 0629 - 636746.

**Hotels:** Rutland Arms Hotel, The Square, Tel. Bakewell 812812.

The Castle Hotel, Castle Street, Tel. Bakewell 812103
The Peacock Hotel, Market Place, Tel. Bakewell 812994
The Wheatsheaf, 5 Bridge Street, Tel. Bakewell 812985
The Milford Hotel, Buxton Road, Tel. Bakewell 812130.

**Cafes:**

The Olde Bakewell Pudding Shop, The Square, Tel. Bakewell 812193
The Smithy, Water Street. The Barn, Bath Street.
Parakeet, The Square. Byways, Bridge Street.Bloomer's, Matlock Street.

**Bus and Coach Services:** All buses leave from The Square daily.The current timetable are displayed.

**Museum-** Old House Museum, Cunningham Place, dates from 1534. Open Easter to end of October. 2 p.m. to 5 p.m. daily. Tel. 0629 - 813647.

**Market Day:** Monday. Fairs held on Easter Monday, Whit Monday and August Bank Holiday.

**Bakewell Show** - established 1819. Held on Wednesday and Thursday in early August. Derbyshire's premier agricultural and horticultral show. Show office Tel. 0629 - 812736.

**Local Newspapers (Weekly):** Derbyshire Times; Matlock Mercury.

**Main shopping area** - Bridge Street, Water Street, Matlock Street and Granby Road.

**Bakewell Factory Shop,** Matlock Street. Tel 0629 - 813110.

**Arts and Crafts-**
Bakewell Cottage Crafts, Butts Road. Tel 0629 - 814271
Sheepsking & Tweed & Gift Shop, Bridge Street. Tel 0629 - 812224
Dragon Designs & Minerals, Water Street. Tel 0629 - 812206
Elf Gems (Blue John Specialist), King Street. 0629 - 814944
Country Life Shop & Country Bookstore (Books and cards), Matlock Street. Tel 0629 - 814333
Country Choice (Outdoor clothing & equipment), 5 Royal Oak Mews, Matlock Street. Tel 0629 - 815212

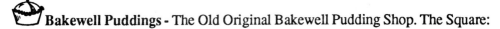**Bakewell Puddings -** The Old Original Bakewell Pudding Shop. The Square: G. E. Bloomer Ltd.. Matlock Street—Bakewell Puddings to original recipe,

**Golf:** Bakewell Golf Club, near former railway station. 9 hole course. Day tickets available.

**Cricket:** Bakewell Cricket Club. Matches played on Rutland Recreation Ground.

**Football:** Bakewell Football Club. Matches played on Rutland Recreation Ground.

**Tennis:** Hard courts on Rutland Recreation Ground.

**Bowls:** The Bakewell Town Bowling Club; green in Bath Gardens.

**Fishing:** Much of the river Wye is private fishing for the residents of the Rutland Arms Hotel, Bakewell, and the Peacock Hotel, Rowsley.

**Gardens:** Bath Gardens; Scott's Meadow; Rutland Recreation Ground.

**Well Dressing Ceremony and Carnival Week -** Held end of June/early July. Tel 0629 - 813241.

*Old Town Hall, Bakewell.*

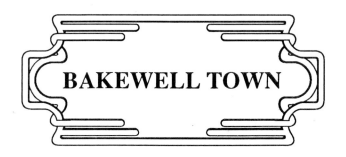

# BAKEWELL TOWN

Throughout Bakewell's history the town has always been an important centre. It is the only place in the Peak District with evidence suggesting a pre-Norman town. Occupying a sheltered site with hills to the north, east and west, and lying at a height of between 400 and 600 feet above sea level the town is a natural creation. To the south is the level valley floor to Haddon Hall. The Bakewell Enclosure Act of 1806 stated that no fences were to be put up in these meadows, only quicksets and drains. It was somewhere in this region, although its exact location is not known, that a Roman altar was found in the 17th century. It is now in the entrance porch of the Banqueting Room of Haddon Hall. The stone dates back to about 150 A.D. and the inscription upon it, translated means:—

*"To the god Mars Braciaca,*
*Quintas Sittius Casecilianus, Prefect of the First Cohort*
*of the Aquitani,*
*performs his vow."*

The first mention of Bakewell is in about 920 A.D. when Edward the Elder, the ruler of Wessex, built a burgh or fortress on what is now known as Castle Hill. The Anglo Saxon chronicle records the building of it at a place known as Badecean Wiellon, meaning Beadeca's Spring, from which today's name is derived. The Romans would undoubtedly have been aware of the warm springs at Bakewell, but, although the Duke of Rutland built a bath house here in the late 17th century, the town never became a fashionable spa town like Matlock or Buxton.

Bakewell is renowned for its market day and is the principal centre for the north midlands. The first recorded reference to markets here is in 1254 when a weekly market and a fifteen day fair were granted to the Lord of the Manor, William Gernon. In 1330 Bakewell became a market town. Today the Monday market attracts large crowds. Approximately 70,000 head of cattle are sold annually and the market is designed to house 600 beef cattle, 1,000 sheep, 128 dairy cattle, 400 calves and 200 pigs.

Much of the history of Bakewell can be gleaned from wandering around the town and appreciating many of the old buildings—Tudor halls, town halls, market halls, alms houses and ancient bridges across the river Wye. The parish church contains a wealth of interest with bosses bearing the arms of various Lords of the Manor and the Vernon chapel with the tombs of the Vernon family. Behind the church, the Old House in Cunningham Place is Bakewell's oldest building and is now a local museum. Water-powered industry has played a major part in the town's story and Arkwright's 18th century mill lies on the northern perimeter, with the Victoria Corn Mill nearer the centre.

The oldest school was founded by Grace, Lady Manners, on May 12th, 1636, and is today known as Lady Manners School. Originally it was intended for the free education of poor children from Bakewell and Rowsley. According to the deeds, Lady Manners instructed that the school master should be unmarried. Should he marry or misbehave, he should be replaced. He was to work from 7 a.m. to 11 a.m. and from 1 p.m. to 5 p.m. and also read prayers at the parish church every morning at 6 a.m. between Lady Day and Michaelmas and at 7-30 a.m. at other times. He received £15 per annum for this, the money being the rent charge of four fields at Elton.

Among the literary visitors to the town was Jane Austen in 1811. Her novel, *"Pride and Prejudice"*, portrays two local places exactly as she saw them—Lampton as Bakewell and Pemberley as Chatsworth. She stayed at the Rutland Arms Hotel. Ruskin wrote in *"Fors Clavigers"*, dated 1st May, 1871, regarding the new railway line in the town (now closed and used as the Monsal Trail) -

*"Now every fool in Buxton can be in Bakewell in half an hour, and every fool in Bakewell at Buxton."*

M. J. B. Baddeley in his guide "The Peak" wrote of Bakewell -

*"A pleasanter-looking town than Bakewell we know not. It distinctly asserts itself without being in any way pretentious. The stream in front and the wooded hills behind are in thorough harmony, graceful and unobtrusive."*

It still is today and I hope your wanderings around the town and its immediate area will uphold the above one hundred year old findings and writings.

# BAKEWELL'S HISTORIC BUILDINGS

A short walk around the centre of Bakewell will bring you to many of these fascinating buildings. Beginning on Bridge Street, there is -

**Rutland Arms Hotel:** Built in 1804 on the site of the former White Horse Inn. It has five bays and a Tuscan porch. The stables to the inn are on the opposite side of the road. William Greaves, the landlord in the 19th century, was among other things *"a Contractor for the Queen's Highway"* and consequently maintained twenty coaches. In about 1859 the cook, by mistake, made the first Bakewell pudding. In 1811 Jane Austen stayed here and parts of her novel, *"Pride and Prejudice"*, can be readily identified with the hotel.

**The Old Market Hall:** Built in the latter half of the 17th century and originally having open arches on the ground floor. The building has been used for a variety of purposes. In 1827 it was the Town Hall; later the ground floor was a wash house and the first floor a courtroom; in 1891 it was a restaurant; and later it became a rating office, dance hall and library. Today it has been fully restored and now serves as an Information Centre for the Peak Park Planning Board.

**Bridge:** Over the river Wye. Built about 1300 with five pointed arches, it was widened in the 19th century.

On King Street and working one's way to beyond the parish church are the following buildings:

**Old Town Hall:** 17th century building with mullioned windows. The hall is famed as the scene of the Bakewell riots following the passing of the Militia Act, which from 1796 led to the Quarter Sessions being no longer held in Bakewell. The following century Lady Manners School used the ground floor while the first floor was a Working Men's Club. This century the fire engine was garaged there, and up to 1964 it was a fish shop. In front of the building was held the Butter Market and the village stocks were also positioned here. The present owner, Mr. M. Goldstone, has restored the building and uses it for his antiques together with the buildings (Avenel Court) at right angles to it with the Georgian frontage.

**Almshouses:** Just above the Old Town Hall are the six . The charity was a gift of the Manners family for six single men.

**Catcliffe House:** Three storeyed mid-18th century building.

**Old House Museum:** At the rear of the church and on Cunningham Place is the Old House. The building, a typical yeoman house with wattle and daub walls, dates back to 1534 and belonged originally to the Gell family. In 1954 it was saved from demolition by the Bakewell and District Historical Society which has turned the building into a museum. Eleven rooms are now open to the public and display approximately 2,000 exhibits—farming, house hold, furniture, clothing, pottery, minerals and craft, with the main emphasis on local items. The museum is open from Easter to September, 2-30 p.m.—5 p.m.

The following buildings are either on the A6 Buxton Road or just off it:—

**Bagshaw Hall:** On Bagshaw Hill. Often referred to as Bakewell Hall, it was built in 1686 for Thomas Bagshaw. Through marriage it passed into the Fitzherbert family and today it is the West Derbyshire Conservative and Unionist Association club.

**Rutland Terrace:** On the A6 Buxton Road, this is a row of four early 19th century houses.

**Bath House:** On Bath Street. Built in 1697 for the Duke of Rutland with a bath measuring 33 ft. by 16 ft. and filled with the Chalybeate spring water, which has a constant temperature of 59° F. The bath is no longer used. The house formerly belonged to White Watson, F.L.S., a noted geologist who wrote the book "Strata of Derbyshire" in 1811. Today it is used by the British Legion.

**Victorian Corn Mill:** The building dates back to the late 18th century and belonged to the Duke of Rutland. Up to the end of World War II the mill was used for grinding corn by the local farmers and the wheels were driven by the river Wye. The mill wheel has been removed by the present owners and can be seen on the right-hand side of the building. It measures 16 ft. in diameter and is 13 ft. 6 in. wide.

On the western fringe of the town are three interesting buildings:—

**Holme Bridge:** Built in 1664 across the river Wye for the pack-horse teams. This accounts for the very low parapet, allowing freedom of loads.

**Lumford Mill:** Built originally by Sir Richard Arkwright for cotton spinning in 1778 when 300 hands, mostly women and children, were employed here. The building was sold in 1840 and was badly damaged by fire in 1868. The mill was rebuilt and the current office block is part of the original building. This century it was used by D. P. Battery Ltd. and is today mostly occupied by W. Fearneough Ltd. The mill had two waterwheels; the largest was 25ft. in diameter and 18 ft. wide and was built in 1827. The smaller wheel was 21 ft. in diameter and 7 ft. wide and was made in 1832.

**Holme Hall:** Attractive Tudor building of 1626 with mullioned windows. On its right-hand side is a terraced, walled garden.

*Castle Street, Bakewell.*

# BAKEWELL CHURCH

Dominating the town and any view of Bakewell is its magnificent parish church, dedicated to All Saints. It is an unusually large building and this is accountable for the fact that there were two priests at Bakewell at the time of the Domesday Book. Later it was a collegiate church when King John gave it to the Dean and Chapter of Lichfield in 1192. There are fragments of a pre Norman church and these can be seen in the foundations of the nave and the supporting walls of the Norman arches. The Norman church was planned on a similar scale to Melbourne church at the southern tip of the county, but the scale was reduced in building. Much of the present church is of 14th century workmanship; the noble octagonal tower and spire were built in 1340 and the Vernon chapel added twenty years later.

The churchyard contains two Saxon cross shafts, including the Great Cross—surrounded by a wrought iron screen—which came from a cross roads near Hassop and is featured in a legend of Prince Arthur (see Customs). The gravestones are worth more than a cursory glance for many contain interesting epitaphs. As you approach the south porch, the main entrance to the church, a tomb on your left to John Dale has the following inscription:—

> *"Know posterity that on the 8th of April in the year of Grace 1757 the rambling remains of the above said John Dale were in the 88th year of his pilgrimage laid upon his two wives. This thing in life might raise some jealousie: Here all three Iye together lovingly, but from embraces here no pleasure flows, alike here all human joys and woes. Here Sarah's chiding John no longer hears and old John's rambling Sarah no more fears, a period's come to all their toilsome lives. The good man's quiet, still are both his wives."*

Before entering the south porch have a look at the west front and doorway built in 1160 and basically Norman workmanship. The south porch contains an exceptional collection of Anglo-Saxon and Norman fragments, which include parts of cross shafts, gargoyles and graveslabs. Many of the graveslabs are 13th century or earlier and by the symbols on them you can decipher the deceased's occupation—sword for soldier, horn for a trumpeter and a bow for an archer. A further collection of fragments can be seen against the west wall of the north aisle.

The octagonal font is 14th century and is from a single block of stone each of the eight panels is roughly carved. Hanging behind the font is a painted wooden shield with the Plantagenet blazon of England and France quarterings. It is believed to have come from Haddon Hall and may possibly have been carried at the funeral of Prince Arthur in the early 16th century as it is of the type then used.

The nave was re-roofed at the beginning of this century and the bosses bear the coats of arms of many of the principal families associated with the Bakewell area through the centuries - William Peverel, Ralph Gernon, the Foljambes, the Vernons and the Manners. One further item of interest in the nave is the monument in the south aisle to Sir Godfrey Foljambe and his second wife Avena. It was made in 1385 and shows half-length figures and in this respect is very unusual. The black marble inscription was added in 1803 and is inaccurate. The Chantry was founded in 1364 (not 1366) by his first wife, Anne (not by Avena).

In the chancel the rood screen is 15th century and among the chancel stalls are six 14th century misericords. Much of the remaining carving dates from the end of the last century. The altar piece of the Crucifixion is believed to be Bavarian and is dated about 1500.

On the right side of the chancel is the Vernon Chapel and one of the most interesting sections of the building. The association with Haddon Hall and the Vernon and Manners families makes the chapel a place of pilgrimage and gives a greater appreciation of the Hall's story. On the right hand wall is the large monument to Sir John Manners and Dorothy Vernon dating from 1584. Underneath their kneeling figures are their children. On the opposite wall is another monument to Sir George Manners, son of Sir John. whose wife Grace Manners founded the Lady Manners School in Bakewell. In the centre of the chapel is the large table tomb of Sir George Vernon, the King of the Peak and the last of the male line, with his two wives. On its immediate left is the monument to Sir Thomas Wendesley who was killed at the Battle of Shrewsbury in 1403.

That, all too briefly, is a little about Bakewell's parish church. It is a building that requires a prolonged visit to appreciate its treasures and splendour.

# CUSTOMS AND FOLKLORE

Bakewell and its immediate area is rich in folklore and customs, some of which are practised today, while the scenes of others can be visited. Firstly, Bakewell itself.

**Bakewell Pudding:** Bakewell is renowned for its delicious mouth-watering puddings, and visitors to the town rarely miss the opportunity of eating one. It is said that a cook in the Rutland Arms, about the year 1859, misinterpreted her instructions and made the first pudding. Mrs. Greaves, the sister-in-law to Sir Joseph Paxton, was the mistress of the hotel. She instructed her cook to make a mixture and put it into a pastry case and spread jam on top. The cook instead spread the jam first and poured the mixture on top. Despite the mistake the diners enjoyed the sweet, giving birth to today's delicacy. Upon Mrs. Greaves death the secret recipe was left to Mr. Radford and was later passed on to a Mr. Bloomer whose son today makes the puddings to the original recipe.

**Bakewell Witches:** In 1608 two reputed *"witches"* from Bakewell were hung in Derby. The tale of their fate is a sad one but reflects the times, for King James I was a highly superstitious man and more than 3,000 *"witches"* were executed during his reign. At the trial of Mrs. Stafford and her sister, the alleged Bakewell witches, a Scotsman informed the court what had happened and upon his *"evidence"* they were found guilty.

Mrs. Stafford owned a lodging house and the Scotsman was staying there. One night he awoke in the early hours of the morning and noticed a shaft of light shining through the floorboards, so he slipped out of bed and peered through the boards at the scene below. He saw Mrs. Stafford and her sister getting ready to go out, suddenly they said: *"Ovl thick, over thin, Now Devil to the cellar in Lunnon."* The lights went out and a whoosh of air carried them away. The Scotsman puzzled and alarmed went back to bed. He lay there thinking about what he had just witnessed an repeated the phrase to himself. Immediately the bed clothes fell to the floor, the windows opened and he flew through the air and landed beside Mrs. Stafford and her sister in cellar in London. They were busy tying up bundles, and . soon as they spotted him they gave him a drink which sent him to sleep immediately. The next thing he knew was constable shaking him awake and taking him to a magistrate to retell his tale.

**17**

**Bakewell Riots:** During 1796-97 there were several riots in Bakewell resulting from the Militia Ballot Act. Bakewell was part of the High Peak Hundred and many people felt that this area was giving more than its quota. Consequently when the magistrate came in 1796 with regard to the Militia, a demonstration was held. Many of the people involved went to see the magistrate and ransacked the room, emptied his pockets and publicly burnt his paper The following year a detachment of cavalry came with the magistrate. A much larger demonstration was held and was broken up by the cavalry, although six men were arrested. After the cavalry left the Roxburgh Fencibles camped beside the town to maintain order, but they were no needed. The Epiphany Quarter Sessions were not held a Bakewell that year and have never been held there again since the riots.

**Bakewell Church:** In the centre of the Vernon Chapel can be seen the large tomb to Sir George Vernon, the last o the male line, who was nicknamed the King of the Peal because of his lavish style of living. One tale still linger about him. Near to Haddon Hall a pedlar was murdered and Sir George ordered that the body be brought to the Long Gallery in the Hall. All his servants and the supposed murderer had to go up in turn and touch the body—*"The Ordeal of Touch"* under which the one who had committed the murder was supposed to shed forth blood. When it came to the murderer's turn he fled and jumped on a horse and rode away furiously. Several of Sir George's men chased him and caught him near Ashford-in-the-Water. They immediately threw a rope over a tree and hung him on the spot. The field was for a long while known as Lynch or Gallows Field. Sir George Vernon was sent for trial in London but the indictment was in the name of *"King of the Peak"* and was therefore quashed.

Outside the church is the Great Cross, originally situated at the cross roads one mile south of Hassop village. Sir Henry Vernon at the beginning of the 16th century was Governor to Prince Arthur, the Prince of Wales. It is reputed that the Prince sat against the cross near Hassop in September 1501 and had a dream while he slept. He dreamt that his bride-to-be was to come across the water, but would later become a widow. The dream accurately portrayed his future. When he returned to Haddon, Sir Henry Vernon informed him that his betrothed, Catherine, the fourth daughter of Ferdinand, King of Castile and Aragon, had landed from Spain. They were married not long afterwards, and within four months of his marriage he died. His last words were *"O, the vision of the cross at Haddon."*

Folklore and customs associated with the immediate area of Bakewell include:—

**Well Dressing:** This is the most colourful of the Peak District customs with the majority of the limestone villages dressing their wells each summer. Ashford-in-the-Water, two miles from Bakewell, observes this custom the week beginning Trinity Sunday. Five wells are dressed with a colourful mosaic of flower petals, moss and lichens pressed into a clay base, and depicting a biblical or topical scene. The actual making of the scene is delicate and painstaking work. The custom, although it has often lapsed during the centuries, originates from the Black Death in 1349 and was revived in 1950. Numerous Derbyshire priests died during the Black Death except at Tissington, near Ashbourne. The five wells there contained pure water and the priests did not contract the disease. As a way of thanksgiving the wells were annually dressed with flowers, thus originating the custom. Bakewell dresses its wells in late June/ early July, annually.

**Funeral Garlands:** Ashford-in-the-Water is one of the few places where relics of this 18th century custom can still be seen. The garlands are made from a thin wooden frame work, covered with paper rosettes, and in the centre hangs either a paper glove or handkerchief. Upon this is written the date, age and name of the deceased person. They were made for betrothed women who died before their marriage day, and were carried in front of the coffin in the funeral procession. At the end of the proceedings the garland was brought into the church and hung above the deceased person's pew. There are three to be seen in Ashford church dating back to the mid-18th century. The last recorded observance of the custom was in 1820.

**The Ashford Dwarf:** Living in Ashford during the 18th century was a very unusual character known locally as *"Mar Bray"* or *"Owd Molly Bray"*. Her height was only three feet and she was known as a very gentle person, although her hygiene left much to be desired. Her attire was described as being "a wide awake hat, an old scarlet cloak or loose bed-gown, a thin handkerchief around her head and chin, and a breasted pinafore—both cloak and pinafore being extremely ragged and jagged at the ends." Over her arm was a wicker basket and she walked with a knob stick. She was buried on March 11th, 1811, aged 85. Her longevity was attributed to her *"indulgement somewhat immoderately in the narcotic weed."*

# THE SURROUNDING AREA

# Villages

**Ashford-in-the-Water** (SK 195698): 2 miles N.W. of Bakewell. This limestone village and surrounding area are of more than usual interest. The river Wye runs along the southern fringe of the village and is spanned by two bridges. The western one is the 17th century Sheepwash bridge, now closed to traffic, and the other bears a stone marked *"M. Hyde 1664"*. M. Hyde was crossing the bridge on a heavily laden horse when a strong wind blew him off his mount into the river, where he drowned. The church, dedicated to Holy Trinity, dates from Norman times and has a Norman tympanum in the porch. Inside can be seen a marble inlaid table which won a silver medal in 1884. Ashford was famous for its black marble, mined in the surrounding area. The industry flourished from the mid 18th century until the beginning of this century, and the table is an example of the work made here. The founder of the industry in 1748 was Henry Watson, and a tablet to him can be seen on the nave wall. Numerous footpaths radiate from the village to Great Longstone, Monsal Dale, Great Shacklow Wood and Bakewell.

**Baslow** (SK 252724): 3 miles N.E. The village makes a good base for the excellent walks in the surrounding grit stone country. To the north are footpaths beside the river Derwent and close to the gritstone edges of Baslow and Gardoms. To the south is Chatsworth Park and Edensor village, all linked together by footpaths. In the village itself is the 13th century church dedicated to St. Anne. The clocks on the tower are unusual. On the eastern face is a square clock with Roman numerals and bearing the date 1759; on the southern face is a circular clock which instead of numbers has "VICTORIA 1897". The clock that was here is now in the tower of Stoney Middleton church. Inside the church on the left is a glass case with a pitch pipe used last century for tuning the organ and a dog whip—the only one in Derbyshire and one of only a handful that survive today. In the 18th century there was an official Dog Whipper of the church. He was paid 2s. (10p) a year for *"Whipping ye dogs out of ye church in* *time for divine service."* On the eastern side of the village is a public car park and just over the Bar Brook is a thatched cottage with the entrance to Chatsworth Park further along the path.

**Edensor** (SK 251699): 3 miles E. Village synonymous with Chatsworth House. Edensor was moved in the 1830s to its present position so that the 6th Duke of Devonshire did not see any buildings from his windows. Most of the village is the design of Sir Joseph Paxton, who was the 6th Duke's head gardener and friend. The church with its noble spire was designed by Sir Gilbert Scott and built in 1867. The interior incorporated part of the earlier church including a large monument dated 1625 to Bess of Hardwick's two sons. The western end of the churchyard contains the tombs of the Dukes of Devonshire and a plaque recording the visit of John F. Kennedy to his sister's grave in 1963. Between these tombs and the church can be found the large tomb of Sir Joseph Paxton. Walks in every direction from Edensor take you through Chatsworth Park—to Bakewell, Baslow, Beeley, Stanton Lees and Rowsley.

**Eyam:** 5 miles N. The renowned village where the bubonic plague ravished the inhabitants for fourteen months during 1665-6. Out of 350 villagers a total of 263 died from the disease. Outside the majority of the limestone houses of the village can be seen wooden plaques recording who died in the house and when. Inside the parish church, dedicated to St. Lawrence, is a plague register of the victims, and the chair of the Rev. William Mompesson, Rector of Eyam during the plague. The churchyard contains the tomb of Katherine Mompesson who died from the plague and a tomb to the Rev. Stanley who helped Mompesson during the outbreak. The Celtic cross is one of the finest in the country. Beside the churchyard are the plague cottages where the first person, George Vicars, died from the disease. Close by are the village stocks, the sheep roast which is the climax to well dressing week at the end of August each year, and Eyam Hall built by the Wright family in 1676; now open to the public.

Other places connected with the plague in and around the village include the Cucklet Delf where services were held in the open during the plague and where an annual commemorative service takes place in late August; the Lydgate Graves of George Darby and his daughter Mary; the Riley Graves where seven members of the Hancock family are buried; Humphrey Merrill's tomb in the middle of a field; and two boundary stones which helped to mark an imaginary boundary line around the village during the plague. One is on the cliff towards Stoney Middleton and the other is north of the village and is known as Mompesson's Well. In the centre of the village and underneath a metal lid is the bull ring, originally used for bull baiting during Wakes week until the sport was abolished in 1835. The Miners Arms nearby records an unusual marriage ceremony. The public car park and toilets are on Hawkhill Road.

**Great Longstone** (SK 201719): 4 miles N. One of the loveliest Peak District villages, with an attractive main street, green and cross. There are several interesting buildings and towards the western end of the village is Longstone Hall. Built in 1747 by the Wright family, who today reside at Eyam Hall, it is classical in style and is built from red bricks. A little further past the Hall can be seen the notice board on the "Licensed Slaughterers" shop. The church is a majestic building on the northern side of the village and dates from the 13th century. The nave has an exceptional roof with moulded beams, dating back to the 15th century. A plaque on the nave wall records the remarkable service performed by Dr. Edward Buxton in the 1820s. When aged 73 he successfully treated the whole village against an out break of typhus. The pulpit includes a pillar of Duke Red Marble, which came from a mine owned by the Duke of Devonshire. Most of its stone was kept in the cellars of Chatsworth House and this is one of the few pieces to be seen. One mile west of Great Longstone is Little Long stone where the stone uprights of the village stocks can be seen beside the road. Just outside this village one can look down from the Peak District's most famous viewpoint—over Monsal Dale and Cressbrook. There is good walking down the dale and there are many paths around Great Longstone.

**Hassop** (SK 224723): 3 miles N. Formerly owned by the Eyres, one of Derbyshire's leading families since the 15th century. The Eyre Arms inn perpetuates their memory and the inn sign bears their coat of arms. Near the Catholic church is a 17th century manor house with mullioned windows. The church was built by the Eyre family in 1816 and is a most attractive building in classical revival style. Inside, above the altar, is a painting of the Crucifixion by Ludovico Carracci. Behind the tall wall opposite is Hassop Hall built by the Eyre family at the beginning of the 17th century. It has had a chequered history, and during Henry VII's reign the Eyres had to pay £21,000 to get it back after allowing it to be used as a garrison by the losing side! It is now a hotel.

**Monyash** (SK 151665): 4 miles S.W. On the village green stands the market cross dating back to 1340 and recording the village's right to hold a market—as it still does at the end of August. Monyash was once an important lead mining centre and in the surrounding area can be found many remains of mining activity. The church dates back to the 17th century and has a 700 year old wooden chest inside. The clock was made by John Whitehurst of Derby in 1805. With a car park on the Bakewell road just outside the village, Lathkill Dale—one of the Peak District's most scenic valleys—is readily accessible. A good footpath leads you down into the dale through a small limestone gorge and rugged scenery. The river Lathkill flows out of a cave entrance. In the summer it is usually dry but in winter time there is a torrent. Nearby is Cales Dale and One Ash Grange which was formerly a penal settlement for misbehaving monks from Roche Abbey, near Maltby in South Yorkshire. Both places are accessible by footpaths.

**Over Haddon** (SK 205665): 2 miles S. Attractive lime stone village commanding a magnificent view down on to Lathkill Dale. There is a large car park on the western side of the village, giving access to the footpaths through the dale. Born here in l651 was Martha Taylor who became renowned as a fasting damsel. During 1669/70 she never ate anything for fourteen months. The whole period of self imposed fast is fully documented and there is little doubt that she starved for this length of time. A rota of two women were by her bedside 24 hours a day and four books by learned men were written at this time about their find ings. She died fifteen years later and was buried on June 12th. 1684, in Bakewell churchyard.

**Rowsley** (SK 258658): 4 miles S.E. On the southern side of the village, two Derbyshire rivers, Wye and Derwent, meet. Facing the A6 road is the Peacock Hotel, dating from 1652. The carved peacock over the porch is part of the crest of the Manners family whose descendants still own Haddon Hall today. The building was originally the private residence of rohn Stevenson, *"Man of Affairs"* to Grace, Lady Manners. the mother of the 8th Earl of Rutland. who was responsible for founding Lady Manners School in Bakewell in 1636. Caudwell's flour mill by the river Wye is open daily with a craft centre. Walks in the area include paths beside the river Derwent, through Manners Wood to Bakewell and onto Stanton Moor.

**Sheldon** (SK 174688): 3 1/2 miles W. Single row of mostly 18th century cottages lining the main street. Numerous footpaths radiate out from the village through surrounding limestone country to Monyash, Flagg, Monsal Dale and Ashford-in-the-Water. One mile west of the village is Magpie Mine. This lead mine was active for some 300 years and is now being restored by the Peak District Mines Historical Society Ltd.

**Stoney Middleton** (SK 232755): 4 miles N. The church dedicated to St. Martin is very unusual with a 15th century tower and an octagonal nave built in 1759. A little further up the lane from the church can be seen the restored bath house, and thirty feet further on can be found the curative spring which has a constant temperature of 63° F. all year round. Approaching the main A6 road from the church you see the toll house, built of gritstone in 1840 at a cost of £87.15s.(£87.75p) and now serving as the fish and chip shop. In the row of houses beyond is the Lover's Leap Cafe. Hannah Braddley, who had been jilted by her lover, William Barnsley, jumped from the limestone cliff above the cafe in 1762. As the sign portrays, her voluminous skirts acted as a parachute and her fall was cushioned. She died two years later in 1764 aged 26.

**Youlgreave** (SK 209643): 3 miles S. During June a well dressing ceremony takes place here. The church dominates the main street and has an exceptionally fine 15th century tower in Perpendicular style. The font inside is unique and has a holy water stoup incorporated onto the side. It originally belonged to Elton church which unknowingly threw it outside; an action it has regretted ever since. Among the other items worthy of interest is a tomb to Thomas Cockayne who died in 1488, an alabaster panel to Robert Gilbert and family, and a 12th century stone effigy of Sir John Rossington. Walks in the area include Bradford Dale and Middleton to Lathkill Dale and the gritstone outcrops of Cratcliffe Tor and Robin Hood's Stride.

*Sheepwash Bridge, Ashford-in-the-Water.*

# Historic Houses

**Haddon Hall** (SK 235664): 2 miles S. A footpath running beside the river Wye from Bakewell brings you to this remarkable building, justifiably called the finest manorial home in England. To visit it is to be taken back to the 16th century. The building spans 400 years from the end of the 11th century when it was occupied by Sir William Peveril, whose castle is situated above Castleton. The Peveril family soon lost their manors through misbehaviour. Later through marriage the manor came into the Vernon family, who were largely responsible for creating the present day house and gardens. The Long Gallery was made by Sir George Vernon in the mid-16th century. The last of the line of Vernons, he was exceedingly wealthy and because of his lavish style of living was nicknamed the King of the Peak. Upon his death his estates were divided between his two daughters, Margaret and Dorothy.

Dorothy Vernon had married Sir John Manners, thereby passing the Hall and manor into the Rutland family who own it today. There are several legends about the Hall but the most popular one refers to the elopement of Dorothy and her husband-to-be, Sir John Manners. Sir George Vernon is reputed to have disapproved of the match. At the agreed time of midnight, Dorothy slipped out of the Hall and crossed the bridge over the river Wye to meet Sir John in the wood. Together they mounted their, horses and rode into Leicestershire, where they married the next day. Monuments to the Vernons can be seen in the Vernon Chapel of Bakewell church.

After 1700 the Dukes of Rutland had moved from Haddon to their newly built Belvoir Castle in Leicestershire. Haddon was rarely visited and by the end of the 19th century it was slowly decaying. One wall of the tower was eleven inches out of true. The Duke at the time was very interested in his ancestral home, and spent some twenty years restoring the building to its former glory. We are ever in his debt for the building is a slice of history rarely found in one place. To wander around the courtyard, the chapel, the kitchens and banqueting hall, the chambers and Long Gallery is a never ending pleasure. The walled gardens, now 400 years old, with their roses, fountains and flowering clematis are a delightful sight in June and July. The Hall and gardens are open from the beginning of April to the end of September, Tuesday to Saturday inclusive, from 11 a.m. to 6 p.m. There is a car park opposite the entrance gate to the Hall.

*The Hunting Tower, Chatsworth.*

**Chatsworth House** (SK 261702): 3 1/2 miles E. Set in a very graceful valley, the home of the Dukes of Devonshire is undoubtedly one of the finest buildings in Europe. The present house is the second one to occupy the position. The first buildings were erected by the redoubtable Bess of Hardwick, who later became the Countess of Shrewsbury in the latter half of the 16th century. She and her second husband, Sir William Cavendish, purchased several manors in the 1650s, including Chatsworth for £500. She began to construct a large Elizabethan building costing about £60,000. It was in this house that Mary, Queen of Scots was regularly "imprisoned" when Bess was her guardian. Queen Mary's Bower, the walled Garden near the river Derwent, was where she often spent her afternoons. A coat of arms can be seen over the doorway at the top of the thirty steps.

The Bower and the shooting tower high above the main building are all that remain of the original Chatsworth. In 1690 the first Duke of Devonshire, as he later became, began building the present Chatsworth. He started the west front and became so engrossed in his task that over the next fifty years he built the whole square. It was left to subsequent Dukes to continue the work, and in the early 19th century the 6th Duke, together with his head gardener, Sir Joseph Paxton, completed the task and finalised today's incomparable masterpiece.

Chatsworth is a place that needs repeated visits to appreciate the magnificence of the interior. The gardens are a never ending joy to walk through at different seasons— to see the daffodils, rhododendrons, bluebells and the autumn colours. The lakes and waterfalls are also of more than usual interest Several footpaths cross the Park adding further to the enjoyment of the area. A visit to Edensor village is a must, for it is an integral part of the Chatsworth story. The house and gardens are open to the public from before Easter to October.

# Ancient Monuments

*Arbor Low
Stone Circle.*

**Arbor Low** (SK 161636): 6 miles S.W. Often called the *"Stonehenge of the Peak"*, this is among the best stone circles in Britain. Believed to have been made about 2000 BC (Bronze Age), the henge comprises a single ditch, 6 ft. deep, 30 ft. wide and 250 ft. in diameter, which encircles 46 large limestone stones and 13 smaller ones. All the stones lie flat and it is a controversial point whether they were ever upright, like Stonehenge or Avebury. There are four stones in the centre, and when the henge was excavated at the beginning of this century the skeleton of an adult male was found beside these stones.

Near to the henge is a barrow known as Gib Hill, Gib being short for gibbet. In the 19th century there was a custom that murderers, after being hanged, were gibbeted in a metal suit at the scene of the murder. The hill was excavated in 1848 and found to be a Bronze Age burial mound. The cist was removed but has now been put back onto the mound. A visit to both archaeological remains makes a fascinating outing. Being some 1250 ft. above sea level, the views over the limestone areas are rewarding. The henge is under the care of English Heritage and is open all year round.

**Stanton Moor** (SK 245635): 4 miles S. The whole gritstone moorland is encircled by footpaths and the surface is covered with heather and bilberries. It is a popular walking area, with distant views, and has a folly—Earl Grey's tower—built to commemorate the reform of Parliament in 1832. The moorland has also much to interest the archaeologist with a Bronze Age stone circle and more than seventy burial mounds of the Beaker folk; many have been excavated.

The stone circle is named the Nine Ladies and a solitary boulder nearby is known as the King's Stone; both are gritstone. A legend states that one Sunday nine maidens and a fiddler came onto the moor to dance, thus causing an act of sacrilege for which they were turned to stone.

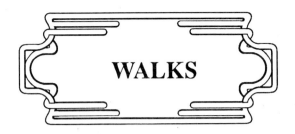

# WALKS

*The 1:25,000 Outdoor Leisure Series O.S. Map The White Peak, covers all the following walks.*

## Short Circular Walks from Bakewell

**Ashford:** *Route: Bakewell—Holme Hall—Rowdale House—Churchdale Hall—Ashford—Bakewell. 5 miles.* From Bakewell cross Scot's Meadow to Holme Hall and walk up the track on the left hand side of it. Half a mile later at a walled track turn left and cross the fields to Cracknowl House and on to the B6020 road at Rowdale House. Turn left and left soon afterwards past Churchdale Hall to Ashford. In Ashford village the church and 17th century Sheepwash bridge are the key features. Return to Bakewell along the path beside the river Wye from the A6 road.

**Haddon Hall:** *Route: Bakewell—River Wye—Haddon Hall—Haddon Pastures—Bakewell. 5 1/2 miles.* From Bakewell walk along the right hand bank of the river before crossing two bridges and walking down the left hand bank to the outskirts of Haddon Hall. After visiting the Hall, cross the A6 road and ascend for half a mile through Haddon Pastures before turning right and heading towards Bakewell. Cross the A6 road and walk through Rutland Recreation Ground into central Bakewell.

**Edensor:** *Route: Bakewell—Ball Cross—Edensor—New Piece Wood—Coombe Farm—Coombe Road—Bakewell. 7 miles.* From Bakewell ascend Station Road and just over the disused railway line follow the footpath to the road at Ball Cross. Continue ahead along a single track road for half a mile before bearing right down a walled lane into Edensor. About 100 yards on the right hand side of the church ascend the steps and cross open fields to New Piece Wood. Follow the grass track directly through the wood and towards Calton Houses. Before descending to the houses turn right and shortly begin going up the field to Manners Wood. Bear left through the wood before dropping gradually to the track beside Aron Hole Plantation. Turn right down the track, then the road, past Coombe Farm and into Bakewell.

# Short Circular Walks in the Surrounding Area

**Chatsworth Park:** *Route: Carlton Lees car park—Carlton Houses—Edensor—Chatsworth Park—river Derwent—Carlton Lees. 3 1/2 miles.* From the car park walk along the road into Carlton Lees. Where the road bends sharp left, turn right and go through the gate and gradually ascend the rough track to Carlton Houses. Go past the houses following a grass track as it curves into Carlton Pastures. Keep straight ahead and go through the gate and New Piece Wood before descending across the open fields to Edensor, aiming for the left hand side of the church. From Edensor cross the B6012 and follow the path to the river Derwent and Chatsworth House. To return to the car park, walk along the right hand side of the river to the ruined mill. Here leave the bankside and ascend to the road and car park.

**Stanton Moor:** *Route: Stanton Moor—Earl Grey Tower— Cork Stone—Nine Ladies' Stone Circle. 2 1/2 miles.* A circular walk around the bilberry and heather summit plateau with distant views over to Matlock and the surrounding area. One can join the path around the plateau from the Birchover or Stanton-in-the-Peak side.

**Lathkill Dale:** *Route: Over Haddon car park—Lathkill Dale—Cales Dale—Calling Low—Meadow Place Grange—Over Haddon. 5 1/2 miles.* From the car park descend into Lathkill Dale and turn right and walk beside the river Lath kill. After a little over two miles in the dale, turn left over the bridge into Cales Dale. Shortly afterwards again turn left, and ascend the dale side before crossing the fields to Calling Low Farm. Continue past the farm and across the field to the left hand edge of Low Moor Plantation, and then cross further fields to the Youlgreave road. Go left and walk down it for half a mile before turning left, as signposted, to cross the fields to Meadow Place Grange. Go through the farmyard and onto the edge of Lathkill Dale. Bear right and descend the track down into the dale, leaving a short climb up your starting-out path to the car park.

**Monsal Dale:** *Route: Monsal Dale Head car park—Monsal Dale—Great Shacklow Wood—Ashford—Longstone—Monsal Head. 6 miles.* From the car park, walk along the road to a sharp right hand bend above the dale. Descend the footpath on the left hand side of the bend. Down in the dale bottom cross the footbridge over the river Wye and walk through the dale on the right hand side to the A6 road. Go straight across and through the car park, as footpath signposted, to the stile. Curve round the field to Dimin Dale and keep straight ahead up a rocky path through the wood and past a ruined mill to gain the Sheldon road near Ashford. Walk along the A6 a short distance before entering Ashford via its Sheepwash bridge. Leave the village via the B6465 and after 1/4 mile bear right and follow the path across the fields to Little

Longstone On gaining the road turn left back to Monsal Head.

**Baslow Edge:** *Route: Baslow car park—Baslow Edge—Curbar—river Derwent—Bubnell—Baslow. 5 1/2 miles.* Leave Baslow by walking up the road past the Cottage Cafe, then Bar Road and on up to the walled track to Wellington's Monument. Cross the moorland to the road at Curbar Gap. Turn left down the road before following a path to the outskirts of Curbar village. Continue descending through the village to the bridge over the river Derwent. On the far side of the bridge turn left and follow the footpath under the new road bridge. Walk beside the river and later across the fields to the road at Bubnell. Turn left and descend gradually back into Baslow. A short road walk returns you to the car park.

**Gritstone Edge:** *Route: Baslow car park—Wellington's Monument—Gardom's Edge—Robin Hood Inn—Chatsworth Park—Baslow. 4 1/2 miles.* Leave Baslow by walking up the road past the Crofters Restaurant, and then Bar Road to Wellington's Monument. Before reaching the monument bear right and follow the footpath underneath it before descending to the A621 road. Cross over and follow another path curving its way under Gardom's Edge and on to Robin Hood Inn. Cross the A619 road nearby and follow the concessionary path through Chatsworth Park, past Chatsworth Edge, and back to Baslow car park.

**Plague Village:** *Route: Eyam (car park on Hawkhill Road)—Riley Graves—Stoney Middleton—The Cliff—Eyam. 3 miles.* From Hawkhill Road, turn left along Church Street to pass the Hall, stocks, plague cottages, church and on to the Square. Keep straight ahead on the Grindleford Road (B6251). On the village outskirts turn left up a farm drive and right where it forks. Shortly afterwards the Riley Graves are on your left. Continue on walled path a little further before turning right and descending through a wood to the B6251 road. Turn right and on the right hand bend keep straight ahead on a walled lane down into Stoney Middleton. From the church ascend the Bank and take the footpath over The Cliff back into Eyam via the Darby graves. Retrace your steps back past the church to the car park.

**Tideswell Dale Nature Trail:** Car park and picnic site. A two mile return walk through a limestone dale, full of wild flowers and butterflies, with a basalt quarry to visit.

# Special offers - including postage and packing.

**John Merrill's Happy Walking Cap** - £3.00
- (all colours - one size fits all)

**I've done a John Merrill Walk T shirt** -£7.50
(all sizes state size - Emerald Green with white lettering)

**Map Case** - as recommended by John Merrill - £3.75

**Happy walking! button badge** - 50p.

Send cheque or postal order to - (Visa and Mastercard accepted)

*El Morro Equipment Ltd.,*
*Milne House, Speedwell Mill,*
*Millers Green, Wirksworth,*
*Derbyshire. DE4 4BL*
*Tel./Fax 0629 - 826354*

---

# BODY HEAT - the personal warming pack. - £1.50

Keeps you warm on the inside when you're outside.

✻ Perfect for outdoor sports and activities.

✻ Generates heat for up to 20 hours.

✻ Convenient pocket size.

✻ Keep one in your first aid kit or car for emergency.

**Body Heat** is great for the outdoors, helping to protect you from the cold, whether you are hiking, skiing, fishing, golfing etc., A great survival aid.
Available from -          *El Morro Equipment Ltd.,*
*Milne House, Speedwell Mill, Millers Green,*
*Wirksworth, Derbyshire. DE4 4BL*
*Tel/Fax 0629 - 826354*

"from footprint to finished book"

CIRCULAR WALK GUIDES -
*SHORT CIRCULAR WALKS IN THE PEAK DISTRICT - Vol. 1 and 2*
*CIRCULAR WALKS IN WESTERN PEAKLAND*
*SHORT CIRCULAR WALKS IN THE STAFFORDSHIRE MOORLANDS*
*SHORT CIRCULAR WALKS - TOWNS & VILLAGES OF THE PEAK DISTRICT*
*SHORT CIRCULAR WALKS AROUND MATLOCK*
*SHORT CIRCULAR WALKS IN THE DUKERIES*
*SHORT CIRCULAR WALKS IN SOUTH YORKSHIRE*
*SHORT CIRCULAR WALKS IN SOUTH DERBYSHIRE*
*SHORT CIRCULAR WALKS AROUND BUXTON*
*SHORT CIRCULAR WALKS AROUND WIRKSWORTH*
*SHORT CIRCULAR WALKS IN THE HOPE VALLEY*
*40 SHORT CIRCULAR WALKS IN THE PEAK DISTRICT*
*CIRCULAR WALKS ON KINDER & BLEAKLOW*
*SHORT CIRCULAR WALKS IN SOUTH NOTTINGHAMSHIRE*
*SHIRT CIRCULAR WALKS IN CHESHIRE*
*SHORT CIRCULAR WALKS IN WEST YORKSHIRE*
*CIRCULAR WALKS TO PEAK DISTRICT AIRCRAFT WRECKS by John Mason*
*CIRCULAR WALKS IN THE DERBYSHIRE DALES*
*SHORT CIRCULAR WALKS IN EAST DEVON*
*SHORT CIRCULAR WALKS AROUND HARROGATE*
*SHORT CIRCULAR WALKS IN CHARNWOOD FOREST*
*SHORT CIRCULAR WALKS AROUND CHESTERFIELD*
*SHORT CIRCULAR WALKS IN THE YORKS DALES - Vol 1 - Southern area.*
*SHORT CIRCULAR WALKS IN THE AMBER VALLEY (Derbyshire)*
*SHORT CIRCULAR WALKS IN THE LAKE DISTRICT*
*SHORT CIRCULAR WALKS IN THE NORTH YORKSHIRE MOORS*
*SHORT CIRCULAR WALKS IN EAST STAFFORDSHIRE*
*DRIVING TO WALK - 16 Short Circular walks south of London by Dr. Simon Archer*
*LONG CIRCULAR WALKS IN THE PEAK DISTRICT - Vol.1 and 2.*
*LONG CIRCULAR WALKS IN THE STAFFORDSHIRE MOORLANDS*
*LONG CIRCULAR WALKS IN CHESHIRE*
*WALKING THE TISSINGTON TRAIL*
*WALKING THE HIGH PEAK TRAIL*
*WALKING THE MONSAL TRAIL & OTHER DERBYSHIRE TRAILS*

CANAL WALKS -
*VOL 1 - DERBYSHIRE & NOTTINGHAMSHIRE*
*VOL 2 - CHESHIRE & STAFFORDSHIRE*
*VOL 3 - STAFFORDSHIRE*
*VOL 4 - THE CHESHIRE RING*
*VOL 5 - LINCOLNSHIRE & NOTTINGHAMSHIRE*
*VOL 6 - SOUTH YORKSHIRE*
*VOL 7 - THE TRENT & MERSEY CANAL*

JOHN MERRILL DAY CHALLENGE WALKS -
*WHITE PEAK CHALLENGE WALK*
*DARK PEAK CHALLENGE WALK*
*PEAK DISTRICT END TO END WALKS*
*STAFFORDSHIRE MOORLANDS CHALLENGE WALK*
*THE LITTLE JOHN CHALLENGE WALK*